First Science

Feel and Touch!

Editorial planning: Serpentine Editorial
Scientific consultant: Dr. J.J.M. Rowe

Designed by The R & B Partnership
Illustrator: David Anstey
Photographer: Peter Millard

Additional photographs:
Chris Fairclough Colour Library 26, 31 (bottom);
E A Janes/NHPA 28;
Ivan Polunin/NHPA 29 (top); ZEFA 29 (bottom).

Library of Congress Cataloging-in-Publication Data

Rowe, Julian.
    Feel and touch! / by Julian Rowe and Molly Perham.
        p.   cm. — (First science)
    Includes index.
    Summary: Describes in simple terms how we feel different sensations such as hot
and cold, or rough and smooth, on different parts of our bodies.
    ISBN 0-516-08132-2
    1. Touch—Juvenile literature. [1. Touch. 2. Senses and sensations.] I. Perham,
Molly. II. Title. III. Series: First science (Chicago, Ill.)
QP451.R67 1993
612.8'8—dc20   93-8214
                                                                                              CIP
                                                                                              AC

First Science

Feel and Touch!

Julian Rowe
and Molly Perham

CHILDRENS PRESS®
CHICAGO

Contents

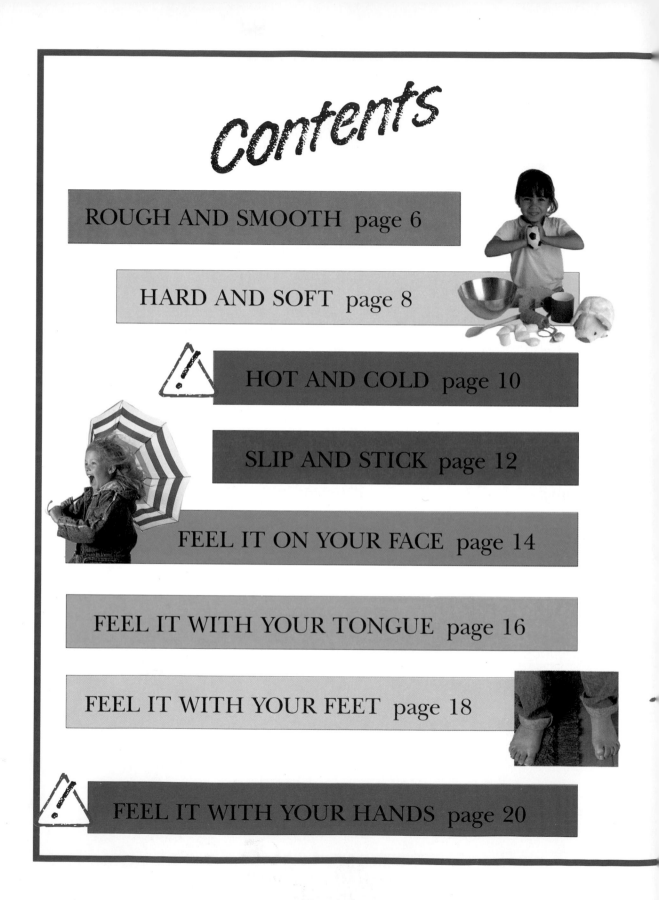

⚠️SAFETY WARNING

Activities marked with this symbol require the presence and
help of an adult. Plastic should always be used instead of glass.

Rough and smooth

You can tell a lot about an object from the way it feels. Collect as many rough things as you can find.

Some may be large, others may be quite small. Some could be natural things, such as a pine cone.

Many things that have been made in factories are smooth to touch. Toys are often made of smooth plastic materials.

See how many different kinds of smooth objects you can find around your home.

Hard and soft

Hard materials are often very strong.
Metal is a hard material.
Metal objects are difficult to break.

But soft materials can be strong, too. The string that is used to wrap packages is almost impossible to break.

How many soft things can you find? How many hard things can you find?

Guess by touch

Materials: A long piece of string and some small plastic bags.

Collect some hard and soft things, such as dried peas, marbles, raisins, cotton, rice, and lentils.

Put each of them in a bag. Tie the bags in a row along the piece of string.

Now ask a friend to feel the bags and guess what each thing is. Remember to blindfold him first, so that he cannot see!

Hot and cold

Some things feel warm and others feel cold when you touch them. You can test how good your body is at measuring temperature.

Fill three bowls with water. Pour cold water into one bowl. Pour warm water into the second bowl and hot water into the third bowl.

Put one hand in the hot water, and the other hand in the cold water.

Now put both hands in the middle bowl,
the one that contains warm water.
What do you feel? Your skin can
feel tiny differences in temperature.
It is very sensitive.

The hand that felt hot now feels cold.
The hand that felt cold now feels hot!

Slip and stick

Make your hands very soapy.
Now unscrew the cap of a plastic bottle.
It's not easy!

Think what it would
be like if everything
felt slippery like that.

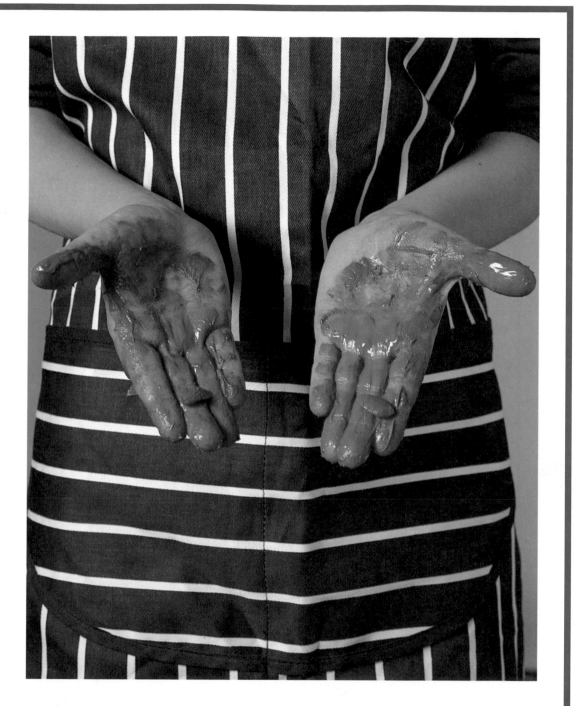

On a hot day, chocolate can melt in your hands—they become messy and sticky. Try it. But be careful what you touch!

Feel it on your face

On a cold day, a hot shower warms you up. On a hot day, a cold shower cools you down. Do you think this boy is feeling hot or cold water on his face?

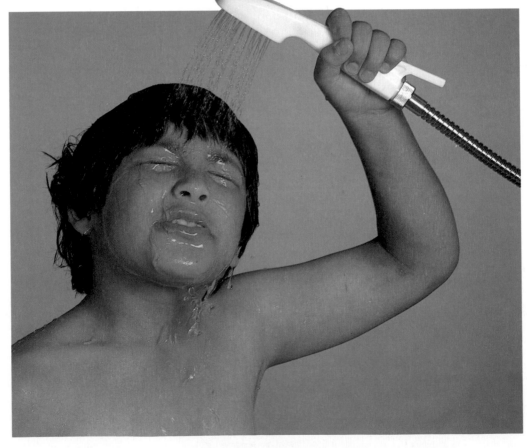

On a windy day, you can feel the strength of the wind on your face. If you are not careful, the wind will blow your umbrella inside out!

Feel it with your tongue

When you feel thirsty on a hot day,
a drink of water tastes very good.
It feels cold on your tongue.

An ice-cream bar
feels even colder.

Have you ever eaten a really hot potato?
Your tongue is very sensitive to hot and cold.

Tasting game

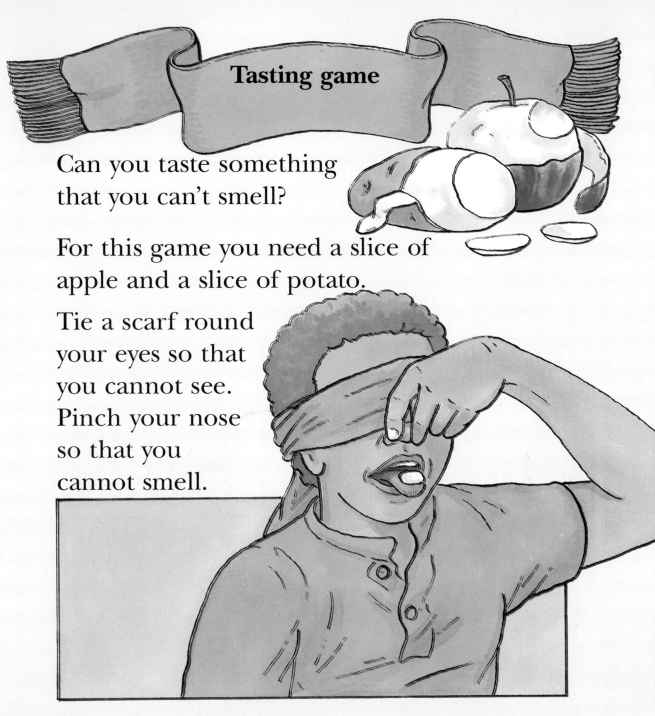

Can you taste something that you can't smell?

For this game you need a slice of apple and a slice of potato.

Tie a scarf round your eyes so that you cannot see. Pinch your nose so that you cannot smell.

Now ask a friend to put one of the slices on your tongue. Is it apple or potato?

Feel it with your feet

Have you ever walked barefoot outdoors?
Your feet can feel every stone and pebble!

The skin of your foot is sensitive to hot and cold. You can test this by standing with one foot on a rug, and the other on a tiled floor.

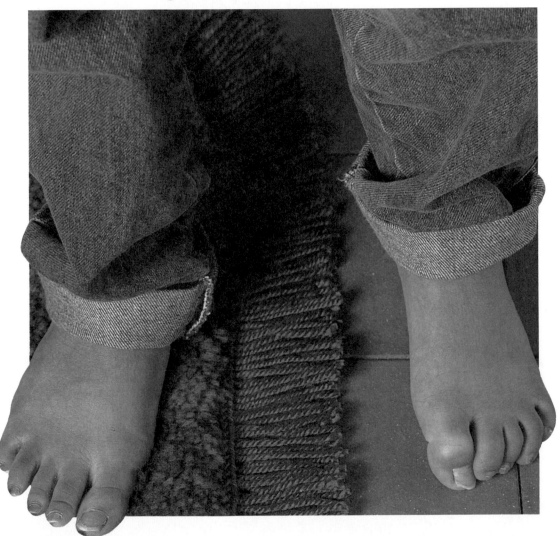

What do you feel? Some materials feel cold to the touch. They are called good conductors. Other materials feel warm to the touch. They are good insulators.

Feel it with your hands

The metal handle of a cooking pan gets very hot, too hot to touch with bare hands. Metals are good conductors.

A wooden handle is not too hot to hold. Wood is a good insulator.

Testing materials

You can test which materials are good insulators.

Materials: Four spoons made of different materials, a bowl, some small candies, and some butter.

Stick a piece of candy on the handle of each spoon with a small knob of butter. Put the spoons into the bowl.

Very carefully pour some hot water into the bowl. Now watch the candies. Which one is the first to fall off a spoon? Is that spoon a good conductor?

21

Using touch

This boy uses his sense of touch to place his fingers over the right holes on the recorder.

When you type on the keyboard of a computer, you use your sense of touch. When you type fast, without looking at the keys, you are touch-typing.

Modeling and shaping

Modeling clay feels soft and squishy when you touch it. If you push in a finger, it makes a deep hole.

You can use your sense of touch to mold the clay into different shapes.

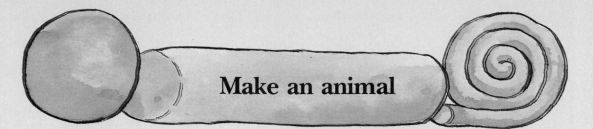

Make an animal

Materials: Modeling clay. Roll a small piece in the palms of your hands to make a round ball.

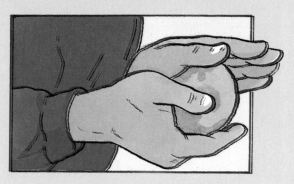

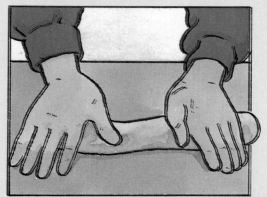

Take a bigger piece of clay and roll it into a sausage shape with your fingers.

Make a third piece of clay into a long, thin roll.

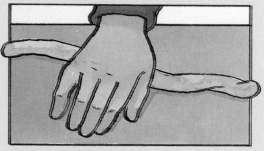

What animal can you make with these pieces of modeling clay?

Touching without seeing

Your sense of touch becomes very important if you can't see. This blind boy is using his fingers to read Braille letters.

Braille letters are made up of tiny bumps in the paper.

Try fastening buttons that you cannot see!
Your fingers feel the button go through the
buttonhole. You don't need to look.

The animal and plant world

The spider waits at the center of the web. It can feel with its legs when a fly lands on the web.

The spider then climbs swiftly toward its prey.

Some plants are
very sensitive.
The leaves of the
mimosa curl up
the moment you
touch them.

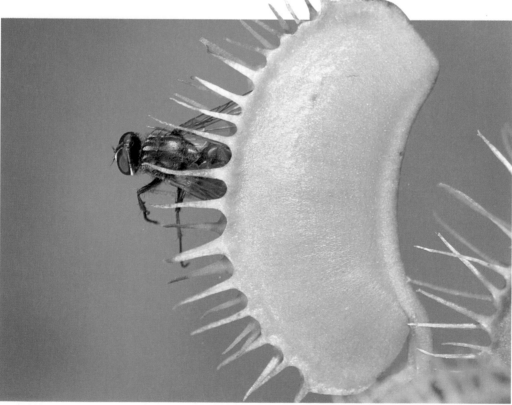

The Venus's-flytrap eats flies. Its leaves close on
a fly the moment it senses the fly crawling on it.

Think about... touch

Can you build a house of cards? If you touch the house too hard, it will all come tumbling down.

Have you ever played pick-up-sticks? Take away as many sticks as you can without making the other sticks move. The player with the steadiest hand wins!

Cover your hands with cooking oil. Now try to grip a soccer ball! The oil makes it slippery to touch. Ballet dancers dip their shoes in a special powder so they do not slip.

When you touch a stinging nettle, the very fine hollow hairs on the leaf pierce your skin. They contain a poison that protects the plant. Bees and wasps also protect themselves with a sting.

INDEX